# Love to Sew

# Hanging Hearts

Rachael Rowe

Search Press

First published in Great Britain 2012

Search Press Limited
Wellwood, North Farm Road,
Tunbridge Wells, Kent TN2 3DR

Text copyright © Rachael Rowe 2012

Photographs by Debbie Patterson at Search Press
Photographic Studio

Photographs and design copyright © Search Press Ltd. 2012

ISBN: 978-1-84448-787-5

The Publishers and author can accept no responsibility for
any consequences arising from the information, advice or
instructions given in this publication.

Suppliers
If you have difficulty in obtaining any of the materials and
equipment mentioned in this book, then please visit the
Search Press website for details of suppliers:
www.searchpress.com

## Acknowledgements

I would like to thank the team at Search Press –
Roz Dace, Katie Sparkes and Marrianne Mercer –
for making writing my first book such an enjoyable
experience, and to Debbie Patterson for taking such
wonderful photos of the final projects.

Huge thanks also go to my wonderful family, for
supporting and encouraging all my creative endeavours
over the past few years; I couldn't have done it without
you all!

Printed in China

Heart Felt, page 20

Name Garland, page 22

Heart of Hearts, page 28

Festive Hearts, page 30

Patchwork, page 36

Baby Hearts, page 38

Button Heart, page 48

Country Style, page 50

*Stitched with Love, page 24*

*Heart Wreath, page 26*

# Contents

*Pretty Pocket, page 32*

*Memories, page 34*

*Sweethearts, page 40*

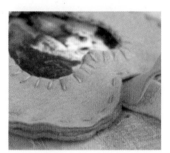

*Puppy Love, page 42*

*Simply Blue, page 44*

*Happy Heart, page 46*

*Flying the Flag, page 52*

*Heart Strings, page 54*

*Rustic Romance, page 56*

*Love Heart, page 58*

# Introduction

Appearing in traditional European art and folklore and on decks of cards since the fifteenth century, the symbol of a heart has represented love for centuries. Its stylised shape adorns countless Valentine's Day cards and is widely used in popular culture. In more recent times, the symbol has moved on to be used as a decorative motif in our homes, with hanging hearts becoming widely available in every style imaginable and on display all year round.

In this book, I show you how to make a variety of hearts to give as gifts, to mark a special day or simply to display around your home, in an array of designs that can be adapted to suit your colour scheme and style. The techniques used are very simple and are explained at the beginning of the book, so even those new to stitching should have no trouble making whichever project they choose.

The twenty projects in this book range from the very simple, though still very effective, to hearts that require a little more time and effort to create something truly unique. Perhaps you want to create a heart-felt gift for a christening, or some festive Christmas decorations for your tree – whatever the occasion, there is a project in this book for you.

# Materials & equipment

The projects in this book use a variety of gorgeous fabrics and trimmings, and there has never been so much choice both on the high street and on-line for sourcing pretty fabrics, ribbons and buttons with which to make a project your own. I have used a mixture of new and vintage fabrics alongside eco-felts and trimmings that can be found in your local haberdashery store. Other than a basic sewing machine with straight stitch, very little specialist equipment is needed for the projects in this book, so you can begin sewing almost immediately!

## Sewing machine

For all the machine-stitched projects in this book, you need a basic sewing machine that is capable of a straight stitch with a backstitch function for finishing off the beginning and end of each stitch line. Use a medium-length stitch and adjust the tension according to the fabric being used.

## Fabrics

I have used predominantly cottons and linens that have been designed for both clothing and interiors. If the project you are making uses two or more fabrics, it is always best to make sure these are of a similar weight and type – this will ensure a more professional looking finish. The felt I have used is an eco-felt created with recycled plastic bottles, and is available at most haberdashery shops in A4-sized squares in a variety of colours.

# Threads

I have used standard polyester machine-sewing threads, available on reels and cones from all haberdashery shops. When sewing a project where the majority of the stitching is functional and on the inside, it is always best to match the colour of the thread to the fabric as closely as possible. For top-stitching detail, you might like to try a contrasting colour for extra interest, though bear in mind this will be far more visible!

For the hand-sewn/embroidered projects, I have used standard embroidery threads/floss, which are available in a huge range of wonderful colours and finishes.

# Pins and needles

For the majority of the machine-stitched projects, where the only hand sewing required is to sew the opening of the heart closed or to sew on embellishments such as buttons, I recommend standard hand-sewing needles. For hand-stitched and embroidered projects, you will require an embroidery needle with a large eye and a fairly sharp point.

When pinning your work, I recommend dressmakers' pins with a ball/pearl head so they are very visible – pin your fabric at right angles to your intended stitch line so you can stitch over the pins without damaging the needle.

# Embellishments

The embellishments used in this book are a very small selection of the wonderful items available in stores worldwide and on-line. I have used a mixture of ribbons, including satin and grosgrain, alongside ric-rac and lace trimmings to create the projects – the choice of embellishments for your own hanging heart, though, is really up to you! The same applies to buttons – mother-of-pearl and rustic wooden buttons have been selected to add to the style of the projects, but you may prefer something brighter and more funky. Again, your local haberdashery store will have a good selection to help you make the projects truly yours.

# Other equipment

You will require toy stuffing to fill your hearts – this is available in bags from most haberdashery shops. You will also need sharp fabric scissors to cut out the shapes in the projects – never use your fabric scissors to cut paper or anything else. You will also need some small, sharp embroidery scissors for trimming and clipping curves, plus pinking shears for some projects. A tape measure or ruler and chalk or a fabric marking pen will also be useful. A stitch ripper/unpicker may also be useful in case of any mistakes.

# Basic techniques

The majority of the projects in this book follow the same basic techniques for constructing the heart shape, none of which require any special skills. You will need fabric scissors, pins and your sewing machine! All the templates for the shapes can be found on pages 61–63 and photocopied or traced to the required size.

## Transferring the template to the fabric

1 Photocopy or trace your chosen template and cut it out. Place the template on your fabric as instructed in the project and pin around the shape. Make sure you place the template on the fabric in line with the grain of the fabric.

2 Cut carefully around the template with your fabric scissors, right up to the edge of the template. Try to use fluid strokes of the scissor blades to achieve a clean edge. Unpin the template and put it to one side.

## Stitching the heart

3 Pin the layers of your heart together according to the project instructions and, starting on a straight edge, sew around the heart with a 1cm (½in) seam allowance. If you are using a sewing machine, use a medium stitch length. Remember to leave a gap of around 4–5cm (1½–2in) to turn the heart through, and backstitch at the beginning and end of the stitch line to ensure a strong seam.

4 Using a small pair of sharp embroidery scissors or snips, clip small triangles into the curved edges of the heart, through both layers. Be careful not to cut through the seam line. Clip the point of the heart to a much flatter shape – this will ensure a defined point when you turn the heart through.

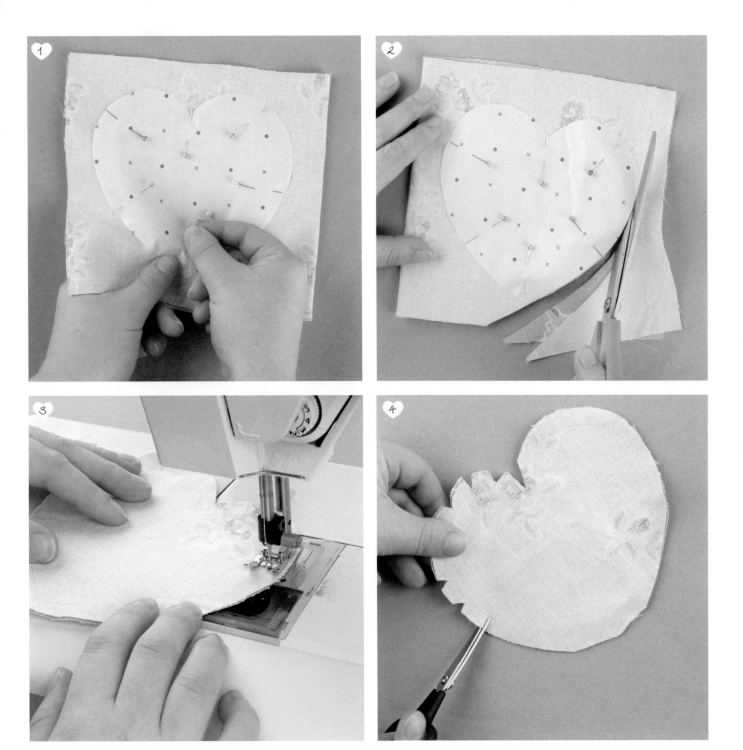

# Stuffing and finishing the heart

5 Carefully turn the heart through so the right side of the fabric faces outwards. Gently roll the seams between your fingers to help create a more rounded shape.

6 Stuff the heart using small pieces of toy stuffing. Using small pieces helps to create a more even shape. Massaging the stuffing into the edges of the heart as you go will help the heart to look more rounded and plumped.

7 Hand sew the opening of the heart closed using a matching thread. Use small stitches and catch only a few threads of the fabric at a time to ensure a neat finish.

8 Your heart is complete.

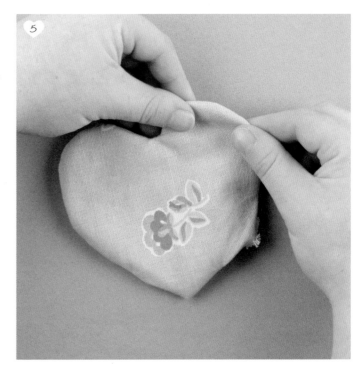

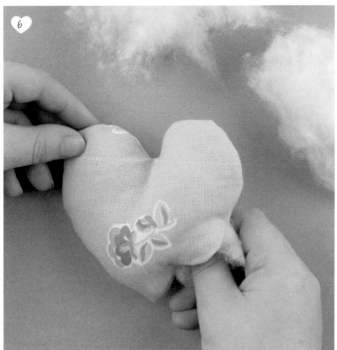

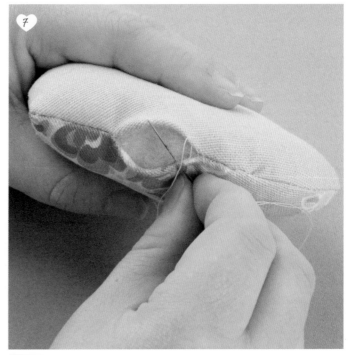

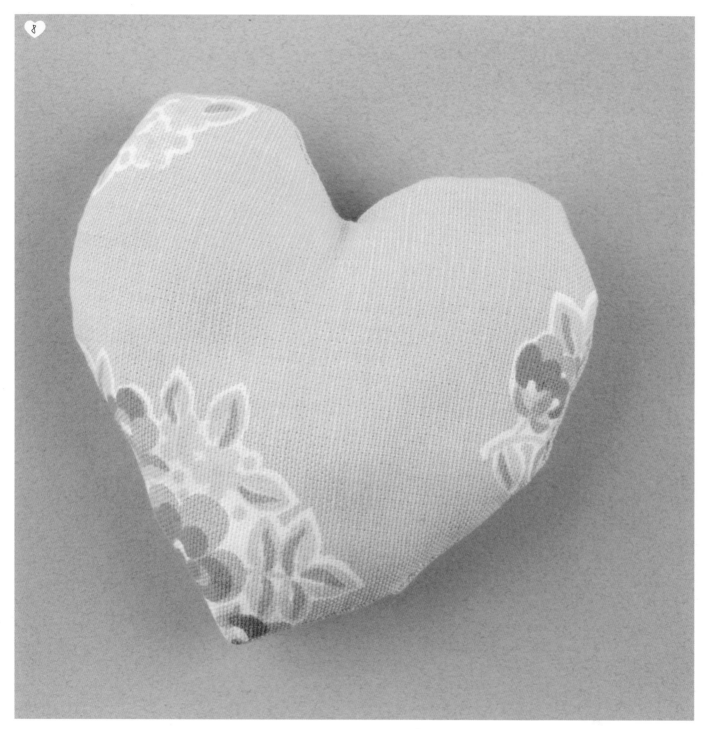

# Hangers

### 1 Adding the hanger to the finished heart

Cross the ends of your ribbon or twine over each other approximately 2cm (¾in) from the ends and stitch the crossed section to the 'V' shape of the heart. Use very small stitches and take care to only stitch through the top layer of the heart fabric. Finish with a button to conceal the stitches.

### 2 Catching the hanger inside the heart – hand-stitched heart

Fold your hanger in half and catch it between the two fabric layers of the heart. Pin it in place. As you hand stitch around the edge of the heart, sew through the hanger, making sure that at least a couple of complete stitches go through the hanger itself to keep it secure and strong.

### 3 Catching the hanger in the seam line – twine loop

Make the length of twine into a loop and knot together. Pin your heart shapes together, catching the twine loop between the two layers with the knotted end sticking out at the top. Sew around your heart.

### 4 Catching the hanger in the seam line – ribbon loop

Fold the ribbon in half and catch it between the two layers of your heart fabric. Pin the ribbon securely in place, leaving 1cm (½in) of ribbon poking above the edge of the fabric. Sew around the heart.

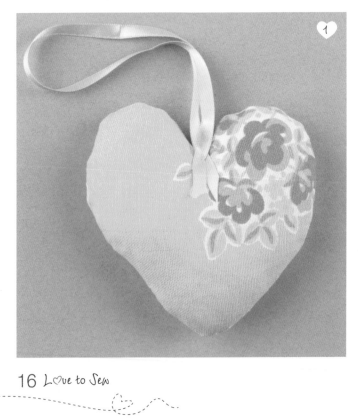

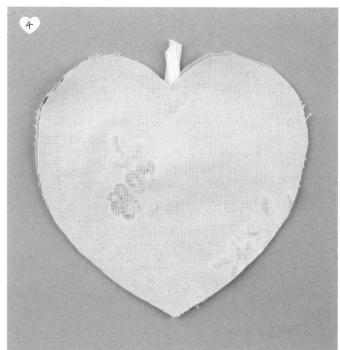

# Projects

On the following pages you will find step-by-step instructions for twenty different hanging hearts. There is a mixture of machine- and hand-sewing projects – perhaps try out a machine-sewing project for almost instant impact when you are short on time, and a hand-sewing project for quieter days. There are simple instructions for the hand-sewing stitches used on page 60, so even if you are a complete beginner you can still have a go!

Each of the hearts is based on one of five standard shapes and sizes that I have provided as templates on pages 61–63. Some of the projects require additional templates that are provided with the relevant project. They simply need to be photocopied, traced or scanned into a computer and printed out. Full instructions for using the templates are provided on page 12.

In each project I've provided a complete list of the materials and tools you need, including the quantities required, and made suggestions for fabric designs and colours that work well together in each project. But of course the real fun will be in choosing your own materials to create a beautiful hanging heart that is not only hand-made, but truly unique.

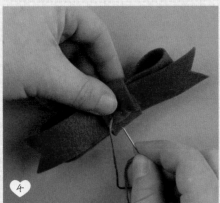

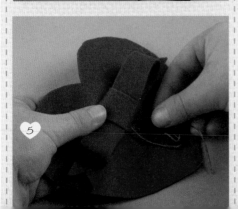

# Heart Felt

## Materials

- ♥ pattern piece B (page 62)
- ♥ two pieces of felt, 17 x 16cm (6¾ x 6¼in)
- ♥ one piece of felt, 23 x 2.5cm (9 x 1in)
- ♥ one piece of felt, 14 x 2.5cm (5½ x 1in)
- ♥ one piece of felt, 19 x 2.5cm (7½ x 1in)
- ♥ one piece of felt, 8 x 2.5cm (3¼ x 1in)
- ♥ contrasting embroidery thread
- ♥ stuffing

## Tools

- ♥ fabric scissors
- ♥ embroidery needle
- ♥ pins

1 Place the two large pieces of felt together and pin on pattern piece B. Cut out.

2 Take the 23cm (9in) strip of felt and fold it into a loop, overlap the ends by 1cm (½in) and sew together.

3 Take the 14cm (5½in) strip of felt and trim the ends into inverted points to represent ribbon. Position the loop you've just made centrally on this piece and sew it in place.

4 Next, take the 8cm (3¼in) strip of felt and loop it around the centre of the two pieces to form the bow. Sew it in place on the back.

5 Position the bow on the centre of one of the felt hearts and sew it securely in place.

6 Place the two felt hearts together, wrong sides facing, and pin. Fold the remaining 19cm (7½in) strip of felt in half and trap it between the two layers of the heart to form the hanging loop. Pin it in place. Sew the hearts together using embroidery thread and running stitch approximately 1cm (½in) from the edge of the fabric, leaving a 4cm (1½in) gap on one straight side. Leave the thread attached to finish the heart after stuffing.

7 Stuff the heart using small pieces of stuffing. Continue sewing until the gap is closed.

# Name Garland

## Materials

- pattern piece B (page 62), copied at 95% to measure approximately 14.5 x 13cm (5¾ x 5in)
- floral fabric, one piece per heart, 25 x 14cm (9¾ x 5½in) and one piece per letter, 8 x 6cm (3¼ x 2¼in)
- dotty fabric, one piece per heart, 25 x 14cm (9¾ x 5½in) and one piece per letter, 8 x 6cm (3¼ x 2¼in)
- iron-on adhesive web (e.g. Bondaweb), 8 x 6cm (3¼ x 2¼in) per letter
- ribbon, 1m (1yd) long for a four-letter name (allow extra for a longer name)
- two buttons per heart
- matching thread
- stuffing

## Tools

- sewing machine
- fabric scissors
- iron
- pins
- pencil, chalk or fabric marking pen

1 Decide how many hearts you need to make in each fabric then, for each heart, fold a piece of heart fabric in half, right sides together, and pin on pattern piece B. Cut out. Lay the hearts out in order, alternating them along the length of the garland.

2 Draw the letters required on to adhesive web – remember to draw them 'back to front'. Decide which letter is to go on each heart and, for each one, iron the letter on to the reverse of the contrasting letter fabric and cut out. Peel off the backing paper and iron each letter on to the centre of its fabric heart.

3 Machine stitch each letter to its fabric heart with your choice of thread.

4 Pin two hearts together, one with a letter and one without, right sides facing, and sew them together with a 1cm (½in) seam allowance, leaving a gap for turning through and backstitching at the beginning and end of the stitch line. Clip the curves and point of the heart.

5 Turn through and gently roll the seams to improve the shape. Stuff the heart with small pieces of stuffing and hand sew the opening closed.

6 Repeat for each heart in the garland.

7 Lay out the ribbon and arrange the hearts along its length. Hand stitch the top of each heart to the lower edge of the ribbon and conceal the join with a button.

3

4

# Stitched with Love

## Materials

- pattern piece C (page 63)
- piece of linen, 25 x 14cm (9¾ x 5½in)
- variety of embroidery threads for hand stitches
- three lengths of embroidery thread, each 25cm (1¼ x 9¾in) long, for hanging loop
- stuffing

## Tools

- embroidery needle
- fabric scissors
- pins

1 Fold the piece of linen in half, right sides together, and pin on pattern piece C. Cut out.

2 Knot the three lengths of embroidery thread together at one end. Plait them together and knot to secure.

3 Take one heart and hand sew your choice of embroidery stitches on to the right side of the fabric, leaving a 1cm (½in) border around the edge. Some suggestions for embroidery stitches are provided on page 60.

4 Place the two hearts together, wrong sides facing. Catch the hanging loop between the two hearts. Pin them together. Blanket stitch around the edge, making sure you trap the hanging loop securely.

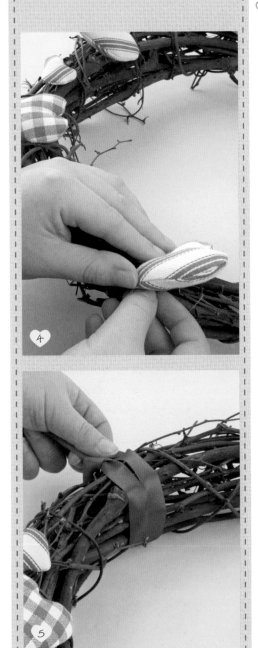

# Heart Wreath

## Materials

- pattern pieces D and E (page 63)
- wicker wreath
- two or three fabrics, quantity depending on wreath size
- matching thread
- stuffing
- ribbon, 1m (1yd) long, to match fabric

## Tools

- sewing machine
- fabric scissors
- hand-sewing needle
- pins

1 Using pattern pieces D and E, fold each fabric in half, right sides together, and cut out the hearts. For this wreath I made six small hearts and six medium hearts, but the number required will depend on the size of your wreath and the density of hearts you want to achieve.

2 Pin the two sides of each heart together, right sides facing, and sew with a 5mm (¼in) seam allowance, leaving a gap to turn through. Backstitch at the beginning and end of the stitch line. As these hearts are far smaller than the other examples in the book, they will be harder to turn through! Clip the curves and point of each heart. Turn through and roll the seams.

3 Gently stuff each heart with small pieces of stuffing and hand sew the openings closed.

4 Arrange your hearts around the wreath, leaving a gap at the top for the ribbon hanger. Hand sew the hearts to the wreath.

5 Tie the length of the ribbon at the top of the wreath for hanging it up.

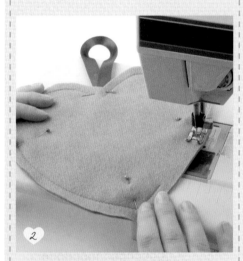

Template for small
felt hearts

# Heart of Hearts

## Materials

- pattern piece B (page 62), copied at 150% to measure approximately 23 x 21cm (9 x 8¼in)
- two pieces of felt, 25 x 25cm (9¾ x 9¾in)
- three pieces of felt in different colours, 13 x 13cm (5 x 5in)
- sewing thread to match the large pieces of felt
- matching satin ribbon, 30cm (11¾in) long
- template for small felt hearts (left)

## Tools

- sewing machine
- fabric scissors
- pins

1 Take the two large pieces of felt and place them together. Pin on the enlarged pattern piece B and cut out. Make a loop with the length of ribbon and sandwich it between the two felt layers. Pin it in place and pin the two layers together around the heart shape.

2 Using matching thread, sew around the heart shape through both layers, approximately 1cm (½in) from the edge, being careful to catch the ribbon loop in the stitch line.

3 Using the template above, cut out nine felt hearts from each of two of the small pieces of felt, and eight from the remaining felt. Working a row at a time, starting from the top, position the small felt hearts in a line of alternating colours across the heart. Pin each heart in place and secure them with a single line of machine stitching through the centre of the row of hearts.

4 Repeat until the entire heart is covered.

# Festive Hearts

## Materials

- pattern piece A (page 61)
- one piece of felt, 40 x 25cm (15¾ x 9¾in), in red or green
- one piece of felt, 10 x 10cm (4 x 4in), in white
- three lengths of embroidery thread in red and green, each 40cm (15¾in) long, for hanging loop
- extra embroidery thread in red or green for sewing hearts together and motif
- tree or snowflake template (left): snowflake copied at 135% to measure approximately 8 x 8cm (3¼ x 3¼in); tree shown actual size, approximately 9 x 6cm (3½ x 2¼in)
- stuffing

## Tools

- fabric scissors
- hand-sewing needle
- pins

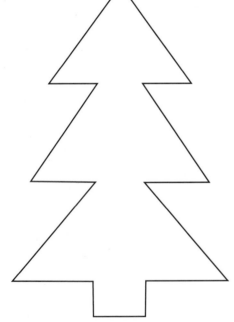

1 Fold the large piece of felt in half and pin on pattern piece A. Cut out.

2 Pin the tree or snowflake template on to the white felt. Cut out. Position the motif on to the centre of one of the felt hearts. Using embroidery thread, hand sew the motif to the heart with a running stitch.

3 Next make the hanging loop. Knot the three 40cm (15¾) lengths of embroidery thread together at one end and plait them together. Knot the end to finish.

4 Pin the two felt hearts together, trapping the hanging loop between the layers at the top. Beginning on a straight side, sew the hearts together with running stitch in an embroidery thread; leave a gap for stuffing, but do not trim off the thread.

5 Stuff the heart and then continue sewing the heart closed.

# Pretty Pocket

## Materials

- ♥ pattern piece A (page 61)
- ♥ floral fabric, 30 x 22cm (11¾ x 8¾in)
- ♥ piece of felt, 30 x 22cm (11¾ x 8¾in)
- ♥ twenty-four mother-of-pearl buttons
- ♥ organza ribbon, 25cm (9¾in) long
- ♥ matching thread

## Tools

- ♥ sewing machine
- ♥ fabric scissors
- ♥ hand-sewing needle
- ♥ pins

*1* Fold the floral fabric in half, right sides together. Pin on pattern piece A and cut out. Repeat for the felt.

*2* Take one fabric heart and one felt heart and pin them together, wrong sides facing. Sew around the edge of the heart through both layers, approximately 5mm (¼in) from the edge. Repeat with the remaining fabric and felt heart.

*3* Place the two stitched hearts together (felt sides facing) and pin around the edge of the hearts. Sew a button on the edge of the heart, just above the point, through all layers. Then sew another button level with it on the other side to cover the stitches.

*4* Continue to sew buttons up each side of the heart, evenly spaced, until you reach the widest part of the shape. Repeat for the reverse of the pouch.

*5* Take the length of ribbon and sew one end near the top of the heart, just to one side. Sew a button over the top to cover your stitches. Sew the other end of the ribbon to the point diagonally opposite on the other side of the pouch to create a handle. Finish with a button.

# Memories

## Materials

- ♥ pattern piece A (page 61)
- ♥ inkjet transfer paper
- ♥ small photograph
- ♥ small piece of linen or calico, 1cm (½in) bigger all round than the photograph
- ♥ small pieces of lace, ribbon and ric-rac
- ♥ four small wooden buttons and a mother-of-pearl button
- ♥ satin ribbon, 25cm (9¾in) long
- ♥ piece of linen, 30 x 22cm (11¾ x 8¾in)
- ♥ stuffing
- ♥ matching thread

## Tools

- ♥ sewing machine
- ♥ fabric scissors
- ♥ iron
- ♥ printer
- ♥ hand-sewing needle
- ♥ pins

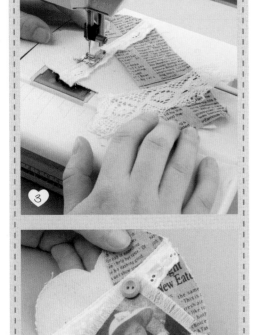

1 Print your chosen image on to the transfer paper so that it measures approximately 6 x 7cm (2¼ x 2¾in). Remember to flip the image, as when it is ironed on to the fabric it will be reversed. Cut out and iron it on to the small piece of linen or calico, following the product instructions. Leave a 5–10mm (¼–½in) border around the image. When cool, peel off the backing paper. Fray the edges of the fabric up to the edges of the image.

2 Fold the large piece of linen in half, right sides together, and pin on pattern piece A. Cut out.

3 Arrange lace, ribbon and ric-rac pieces on the right side of one heart. Pin and sew them in place.

4 Position the image in the centre of the heart and hand stitch it in place with tiny stitches. Attach a button at the corners if you like.

5 Pin the two hearts together, right sides facing, and sew around the shape with a 1cm (½in) seam allowance. Leave a 5cm (2in) gap for turning through. Backstitch at beginning and end of the stitch line. Clip the curves and the point of the heart and turn through.

6 Gently roll the seams to improve the appearance of the heart and stuff it with small pieces of stuffing. Hand sew the opening closed. Make the length of ribbon into a loop and position it at the top of the heart. Hand sew it in place and top with a mother-of-pearl button.

# Patchwork

## Materials

- pattern piece A (page 61)
- satin ribbon, 30cm (11¾in) long
- two contrasting fabrics, each 40 x 25cm (15¾ x 9¾in)
- matching sewing thread
- wooden button
- stuffing

## Tools

- fabric scissors
- ruler
- fabric marker
- pins
- sewing machine
- hand-sewing needle
- iron

1 Using the fabric marker and ruler, divide each piece of fabric into 5cm (2in) squares. You should have 40 squares per piece of fabric.

2 Pin together one square of each fabric, right sides together. Sew down one side with a 1cm (½in) seam allowance, backstitching at the beginning and end of the stitch line. Add another square and repeat until you have a piece eight squares long. Make sure the fabrics alternate. Press all the seams to one side.

3 Repeat step 2 until you have ten strips of eight squares. Next, pin together two strips along the long sides, right sides together, making sure the first squares of each strip are different. Pin carefully to ensure that the seam lines match. Sew with a 1cm (½in) seam allowance and press the seam to one side.

4 Add three further strips, one by one, until you have a piece eight squares by five squares. Then repeat to create a second piece. Position and pin pattern piece A on to one piece of your patchwork fabric and cut out. Repeat with the other piece. Pin the heart pieces together, right sides facing, and sew with a 1cm (½in) seam allowance, leaving a 5cm (2in) gap for turning through on one of the straight sides. Remember to backstitch at both ends of the stitch line.

5 Clip the curves and point of the heart. Turn the heart through and carefully roll the seams between your fingers to improve the shape. Stuff with small pieces of stuffing and hand sew the opening closed.

6 Take the length of ribbon and make a loop. Carefully hand sew it to the heart and top with a wooden button.

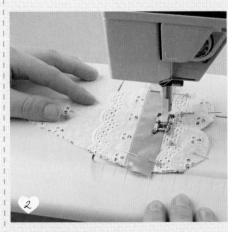

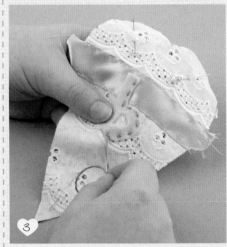

# Baby Hearts

## Materials

- ♥ pattern piece A (page 61)
- ♥ broderie-anglaise fabric, 30 x 22cm (11¾ x 8¾in)
- ♥ pink or blue patterned fabric, 30 x 22cm (11¾ x 8¾in)
- ♥ pink or blue felt, 10 x 7cm (4 x 2¾in)
- ♥ piece of pink or blue ribbon for decorating heart
- ♥ matching ribbon, 25cm (9¾in) long, for hanger
- ♥ button
- ♥ stuffing
- ♥ embroidery thread in pink or blue
- ♥ matching thread

## Tools

- ♥ sewing machine
- ♥ fabric scissors
- ♥ hand-sewing needle
- ♥ embroidery needle
- ♥ pins

1 Fold the patterned fabric in half, right sides together, and pin on pattern piece A. Cut out. Repeat with the broderie-anglaise fabric.

2 Take one heart of patterned fabric and one heart of broderie-anglaise and place the broderie-anglaise heart on top so that the pattern on the fabric can be seen through the holes. Tack together. Repeat with the remaining two hearts. Arrange the length of decorative ribbon across the front of one heart and sew it in place.

3 Cut out an initial of your choice from the felt, pin it over the ribbon and stitch it in place with a running stitch in matching embroidery thread.

4 Take the remaining heart and pin it to the first one, right sides together, leaving a gap for turning through. Backstitch at the beginning and end of the stitch line. Clip the curves and point of the heart.

5 Turn through and roll the seams gently to improve the shape of the heart. Stuff with small pieces of stuffing and hand sew the opening closed. Position the 25cm (9¾in) length of ribbon in a loop at the top of the heart and hand sew it in place. Top with a button.

# Sweethearts

## Materials

- ♥ pattern piece C (page 63)
- ♥ two pieces of fabric, 25 x 14cm (9¾ x 5½in) and 5 x 11cm (2 x 4¼in)
- ♥ stuffing
- ♥ twine, 25cm (9¾in) long
- ♥ matching thread

## Tools

- ♥ sewing machine
- ♥ fabric scissors
- ♥ small, sharp embroidery scissors
- ♥ hand-sewing needle
- ♥ pins

1 Fold the large piece of fabric in half, right sides together, and pin on pattern piece C. Cut out.

2 Take one heart and place the small piece of fabric across it at the widest point. Pin in place. Machine stitch five straight lines across the fabric at equal intervals. Backstitch at the beginning and end of each line.

3 Take a pair of sharp embroidery scissors and carefully cut between the lines of stitching. This line needs to be as straight and possible and centred between the stitch lines.

4 Gently fray the fabric each side of the stitch line, being careful not to go right up to the stitch line.

5 Take the twine and form a loop, knotting the ends together. Place two heart shapes together, right sides facing, and pin, catching the twine loop between the two layers. Sew around the shape with a 1cm (½in) seam allowance, leaving a gap for turning through and backstitching at the beginning and end of the stitch line.

6 Clip the curves and the point of the heart and turn through. Gently roll the seams between your fingers to improve the shape of the heart and stuff with small pieces of stuffing. Hand sew the opening closed.

*The alternative version shown opposite was made using pattern piece A (page 61) and covering the whole of the heart in frayed fabric strips. A ribbon hanger was added to the finished heart and decorated with a button.*

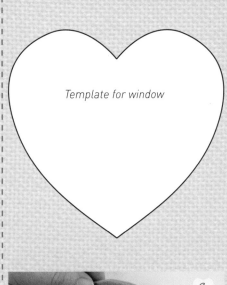

*Template for window*

# Puppy Love

## Materials

- pattern piece B (page 62)
- four pieces of felt, 17 x 16cm (6¾ x 6¼in)
- one piece of felt, 19 x 2.5cm (7½ x 1in)
- contrasting embroidery thread
- template (left) copied at 125% to measure approximately 7.5 x 7cm (3 x 2¾in)
- one or two photographs, measuring 1.5cm (½in) larger than template all round

## Tools

- fabric scissors
- embroidery needle
- pins

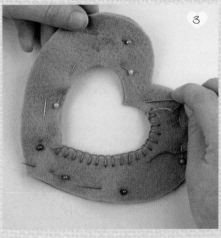

1 Place two of the large pieces of felt together and pin on pattern piece B. Cut out. Remove the pattern piece and pin the shapes back together. Pin the template shown left into the centre and cut carefully through both layers of felt so that you have a heart-shaped window within the larger heart.

2 If you are making a double-sided frame, repeat step 1 with the other two large pieces of felt; otherwise just cut out two of pattern piece B (with no heart-shaped window).

3 Using a contrasting embroidery thread, hand sew a blanket stitch around the heart-shaped window in one or both of the hearts.

4 Next, prepare your photographs. Remember they need to be approximately 1.5cm (½in) larger than the heart-shaped window all round. If you are using two photographs, remember to place them back to back – you may want to stick them together.

5 Take your felt hearts and slide your photograph(s) between the two layers. At this point, fold the 19cm (7½in) length of felt in half to make a hanging loop and sandwich it between the two sides of your frame. Pin in place.

6 Using the contrasting embroidery thread, sew a running stitch around the edge of the heart, through all layers, approximately 5mm (¼in) from the edge.

# Simply Blue

## Materials

- pattern piece A (page 61)
- piece of fabric, 30 x 22cm (11¾ x 8¾in)
- two wooden buttons
- grosgrain ribbon, one piece 12.5cm (5in) long and one piece 26cm (10¼in) long for loop
- two pieces of ric-rac, each 12.5cm (5in) long
- matching thread
- stuffing

## Tools

- sewing machine
- fabric scissors
- hand-sewing needle
- pins

1 Fold the fabric in half, right sides together. Pin on pattern piece A and cut out. Take one heart and pin the short piece of grosgrain ribbon across the width of the heart. Sew down each long edge of the ribbon, remembering to sew in the same direction to prevent puckering.

2 Position the first piece of ric-rac along the top of the ribbon, pin and sew in place down the centre of the ric-rac. Repeat with the second piece of ric-rac along the bottom edge of the ribbon.

3 Place the two heart shapes right sides together and pin. Sew around the shape with a 1cm (½in) seam allowance, leaving a 5cm (2in) gap on one straight side for turning through. Remember to backstitch at the beginning and end of the stitch line. Clip the curves and the point of the heart and turn through. Gently roll the seams between your fingers to improve the shape and stuff the heart with small pieces of stuffing. Hand sew the opening closed.

4 Position the long piece of ribbon for the loop and sew it in place with small hand stitches. Sew a wooden button on each side of the heart to cover the stitches. Trim the ends of the ribbon to a neat point.

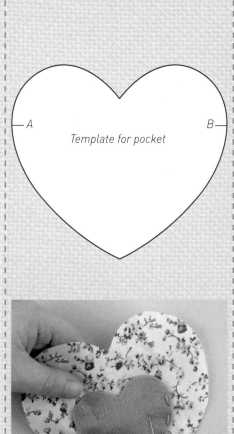

*Template for pocket*

A        B

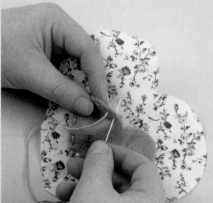

# Happy Heart

## Materials

- ♥ pattern piece B (page 62), copied at 85% to measure approximately 13 x 12cm (5 x 4¾in)
- ♥ floral fabric, 25 x 14cm (9¾ x 5½in)
- ♥ template (left), copied at 150% to measure approximately 9 x 7cm (3½ x 2¾in)
- ♥ matching felt, 10 x 8cm (4 x 3¼in)
- ♥ embroidery thread in contrasting colour to felt
- ♥ ribbon, 25cm (9¾in) long
- ♥ four wooden buttons
- ♥ stuffing
- ♥ matching thread

## Tools

- ♥ sewing machine
- ♥ fabric scissors
- ♥ hand-sewing needle
- ♥ embroidery needle
- ♥ pins

1 Fold the floral fabric in half, right sides together, and pin on pattern piece B. Cut out. Pin the template (top left) to the felt and cut out.

2 To create the pocket, position the felt heart on the right side of one fabric heart and pin it in place. Using the contrasting embroidery thread, stitch the felt heart to the fabric heart with running stitch. Start at point B and continue round to point A. At this point, continue stitching, but through the felt layer only and not through the fabric. Continue to the end and knot.

3 Place the two fabric hearts right sides together and pin. Sew them together with a 1cm (½in) seam allowance, leaving a 5cm (2in) gap for turning through. Remember to backstitch at the beginning and end of the stitch line. Clip the curves and the point of the heart. Turn through and roll the seams gently to create a rounded shape.

4 Stuff the heart with small pieces of stuffing and hand sew the opening closed.

5 Position the ribbon at the top of the heart (as shown in the photograph) and sew it in place. Sew buttons over the top of the ribbon on the front and back of the heart.

*The pocket can be used to store little gifts for your loved ones – sweets, perhaps, or a special ring ...*

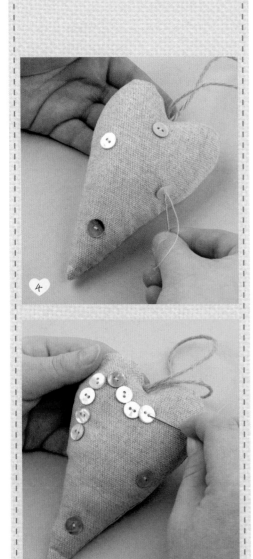

# Button Heart

## Materials

- pattern piece A (page 61)
- piece of linen, 30 x 22cm (11¾ x 8¾in)
- twine, 35cm (13¾in) long
- small mother-of-pearl buttons
- stuffing
- matching sewing thread

## Tools

- sewing machine
- hand-sewing needle
- pins
- fabric scissors

1 Fold the linen in half, right sides together, and pin on pattern piece A. Cut out.

2 Make the twine into a loop and knot the ends together. Pin the two heart shapes together, right sides facing, and trap the twine loop between the layers with the knotted end sticking out of the top. Sew the hearts together with a 1cm (½in) seam allowance, leaving a 5cm (2in) gap for turning on one straight side. Remember to backstitch at the beginning and end of the stitch line. Clip the curves and the point of the heart.

3 Turn through and roll the seams gently to improve the shape. Stuff with small pieces of stuffing and hand sew the opening closed.

4 Sew the first button approximately 2cm (¾in) below the twine loop. Sew a second button at the point of the heart. Sew a third and a fourth button at the midway point on each side to create a framework.

5 Fill in the rest of the outline with buttons, making sure you keep approximately 2cm (¾) from the seam line of the heart.

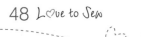

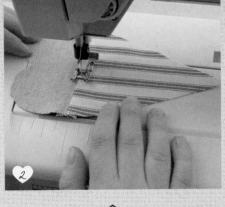

# Country Style

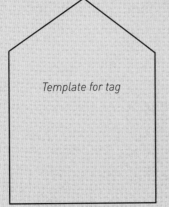

*Template for tag*

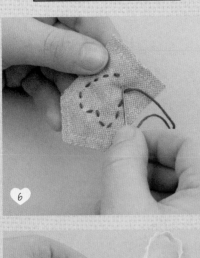

## Materials

- three copies of pattern piece A (page 61)
- ticking, one piece 14 x 22cm (5½ x 8¾in) and one piece 14 x 16cm (5½ x 6¼in)
- linen, one piece 14 x 9cm (5½ x 3½in) and one piece 9 x 7cm (3½ x 2¾in)
- one wooden button
- coordinating ric-rac, 22cm (8¾in) long
- matching sewing thread
- embroidery thread to match ticking
- stuffing
- tag template (left), shown actual size

## Tools

- sewing machine
- embroidery thread
- fabric scissors
- hand-sewing needle and embroidery needle
- pins
- iron

1 Pin pattern piece A to the large piece of ticking and cut out. Cut the top of the heart from the second copy of pattern piece A, down to line B, pin it to the larger piece of linen and cut out. Cut the bottom of the heart from the third copy of pattern piece A, up to line A, pin it to the remaining piece of ticking and cut out.

2 Pin the top of the heart to the bottom, right sides facing, along the straight edge and sew together with a 1cm (½in) seam allowance to form the heart shape. Press the seam open and topstitch each side of the seam approximately 2mm (⅛in) from the seam line.

3 Pin the two heart shapes together, right sides facing, and sew around with a 1cm (½in) seam allowance, leaving a 5cm (2in) gap on one straight side for turning through. Be sure to backstitch at the beginning and end of the stitch line. Clip the curves and point of the heart and turn through.

4 Gently roll the seams of the heart to improve the shape. Stuff the heart with small pieces of stuffing and hand sew the opening closed.

5 To make the tag, fold the remaining piece of linen in half, wrong sides together, and pin on the template (above left). Cut out and pin together. Machine sew the two shapes together, approximately 5mm (¼in) from the edge.

6 Hand sew your choice of motif on to the tag with embroidery thread using a running stitch. Position the tag on the heart and fix it in place with several small hand stitches. Position two ends of the ric-rac over the top and hand stitch in place. Top off with the wooden button, hiding all the rough edges.

*Use the same techniques to make the flag of your choice – I've also made the Stars and Stripes, especially for our American cousins!*

# Flying the Flag

## Materials

- ♥ pattern piece B (page 62)
- ♥ denim/dark blue fabric, 37 x 16cm (14½ x 6¼in)
- ♥ four strips of cream/neutral fabric, 16 x 3cm (6¼ x 1¼in)
- ♥ four strips red fabric, 16 x 1.5cm (6¼ x ½in)
- ♥ red ribbon, 3mm (¼in) wide, 25cm (9¾in) long
- ♥ mother-of-pearl button
- ♥ coordinating sewing threads in red, cream and blue
- ♥ stuffing

## Tools

- ♥ sewing machine
- ♥ fabric scissors
- ♥ hand-sewing needle
- ♥ pins

1 Fold the denim/dark blue fabric in half, right sides together, and pin on pattern piece B. Cut out.

2 Take one of the denim hearts and pin a strip of cream fabric diagonally across the heart. Sew it in place down each side of the strip approximately 5mm (¼in) from the edge. Backstitch at the beginning and end of the stitch line. Fray the long edges slightly. Repeat with a second strip of cream fabric placed on the other diagonal.

3 Change to a red thread on your sewing machine. Position and pin a strip of the red fabric down the centre of one of the diagonal strips. Sew it in place down each long side. Repeat for the other diagonal with a second strip of red fabric.

4 Change back to cream thread and position a strip of cream fabric vertically down the centre of the heart. Sew it in place down each side, 5mm (¼in) from each edge. Fray slightly. Repeat with the final cream strip across the horizontal of the heart.

5 Change back to red thread again and sew the remaining strips of red fabric to the cream strips, as in step 3.

6 Take the remaining blue heart and place the two heart shapes right sides together. Pin together and sew with a 1cm (½in) seam allowance, leaving a 5cm (2in) gap on one straight side for turning through. Clip the curves and point of the heart. Turn through. Gently roll the seams between your fingers to improve the shape and stuff the heart with small pieces of stuffing.

7 Hand sew the opening closed with small stitches. Trim any loose threads. Make a loop with the length of ribbon and sew it in place, adding a mother-of-pearl button on top of the stitches.

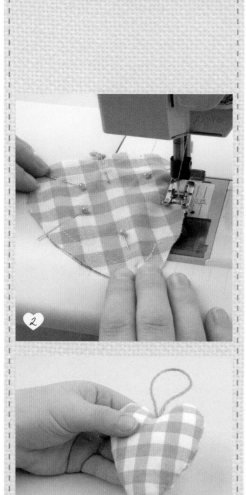

# Heart Strings

## Materials

- pattern piece C (page 63)
- one piece of fabric, 25 x 14cm (9¾ x 5½in), per heart
- twine, 25cm (9¾in) long per heart
- matching thread
- stuffing

## Tools

- sewing machine
- fabric scissors
- pins
- hand-sewing needle

1 Fold the fabric in half, right sides together. Pin on pattern piece C and cut out. Repeat for as many hearts as you need.

2 Make the length of twine into a loop and knot the ends together. Pin two hearts together, right sides facing, and catch the loop between the layers, making sure the knot sticks out at the top of the heart. Sew around the heart shape with a 1cm (½in) seam allowance, leaving a gap for turning through. Backstitch at the beginning and end of the stitch line.

3 Clip the curves and trim the point. Turn through and roll the seams gently to improve the shape of the heart. Stuff with small pieces of stuffing and hand sew the opening closed. Repeat for all the other hearts.

4 To attach the hearts in a string, first stitch the twine loop of one heart to the base of another heart using small stitches worked on the spot. Repeat for the rest of the hearts in the string.

Template for felt heart

# Rustic Romance

## Materials

- pattern piece C (page 63)
- template (left), shown actual size
- one piece of fabric, 25 x 14cm (9¾ x 5½in)
- one piece of coordinating felt, 4 x 4cm (1½in x 1½in)
- one wooden button
- twine, 25cm (9¾in) long
- coordinating embroidery thread
- stuffing
- thread to match button

## Tools

- pinking shears
- fabric scissors
- embroidery needle
- hand-sewing needle
- pins

1 Fold the fabric in half, right sides together, and pin on pattern piece C. Cut out with pinking shears. Pin the template on to the felt and cut out with fabric scissors.

2 Position the felt heart on to the centre of one of the fabric heart pieces. Pin in place and hand sew with running stitch in coordinating embroidery thread. Sew the wooden button on to the felt heart with thread to match the button.

3 Make a loop with the twine and knot the ends together. Pin the fabric hearts together, wrong sides facing, trapping the twine loop between the pieces (keep the knot inside the heart).

4 Sew the heart together using embroidery thread and running stitch approximately 1cm (½in) from the edge of the fabric, leaving a 4cm (1½in) gap on one straight side. Leave the thread attached to finish the heart after stuffing. Stuff the heart using small pieces of stuffing. Continue sewing until the gap is closed.

# Love Heart

## Materials

- ♥ pattern piece B (page 62)
- ♥ floral fabric, 37 x 16cm (14½ x 6¼in)
- ♥ small pieces of lace, ric-rac and ribbon, long enough to fit across the heart
- ♥ satin ribbon, 28cm (11in) long
- ♥ three or more wooden buttons
- ♥ stuffing
- ♥ matching thread

## Tools

- ♥ sewing machine
- ♥ fabric scissors
- ♥ hand-sewing needle
- ♥ pins

1 Fold the floral fabric in half, right sides together. Pin on pattern piece B and cut out.

2 Take one heart and arrange the pieces of ribbon, lace and ric-rac across the shape at different angles. Pin in place and sew in matching thread.

3 Pin the two heart pieces together, right sides facing, and sew around the shape with a 1cm (½in) seam allowance, leaving a gap for turning through and backstitching at the beginning and end of the stitch line.

4 Clip the curves and point of the heart and turn through. Roll the seams gently to improve the shape and stuff with small pieces of stuffing. Hand sew the opening closed.

5 Sew on a button (or buttons) for decorative detail. Position the ribbon for the hanging loop, following the photograph for guidance, and sew it in place with small stitches. Place buttons over the top of the stitches and sew in place. Trim the ends of the ribbon to neat points.

# Stitches

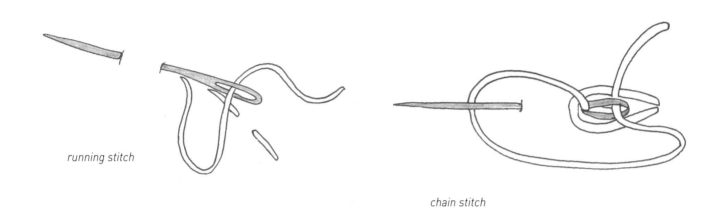

*running stitch*

*chain stitch*

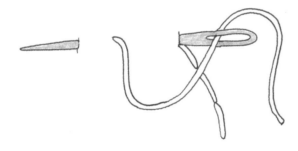

*backstitch*

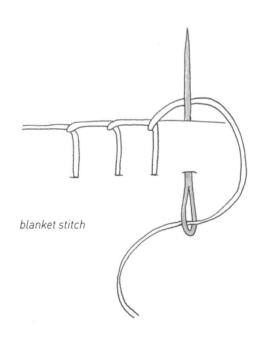

*blanket stitch*

# Templates

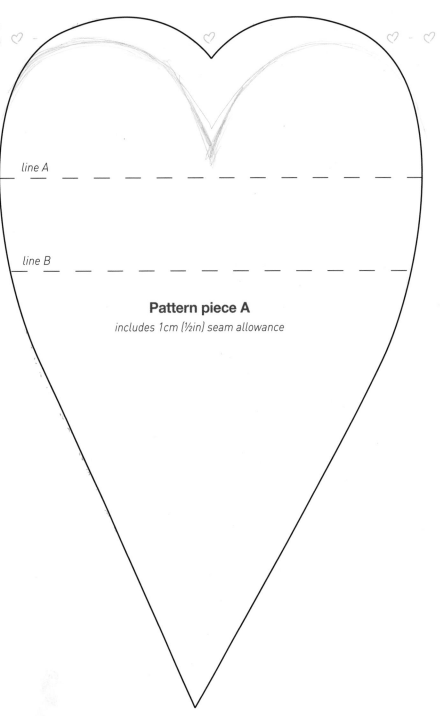

line A

line B

**Pattern piece A**
*includes 1cm (½in) seam allowance*

**Pattern piece B**

*includes 1cm (½in) seam allowance*

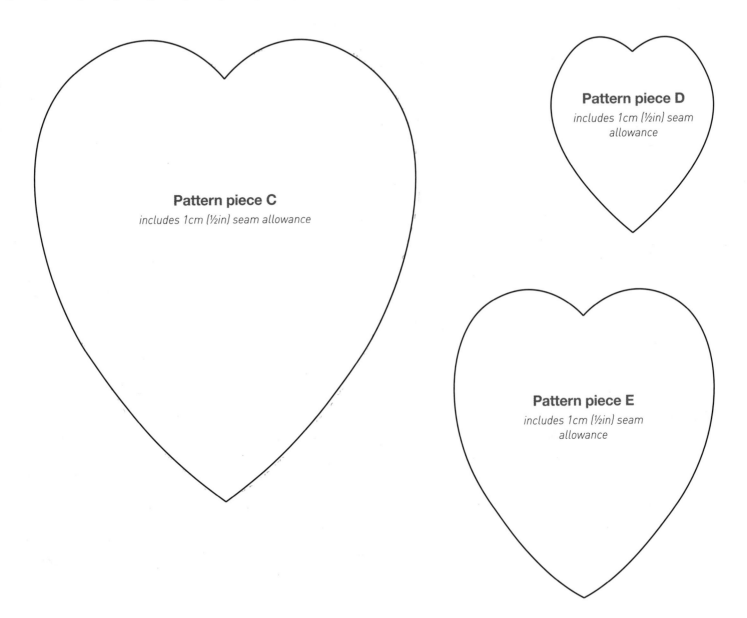

**Pattern piece C**
*includes 1cm (½in) seam allowance*

**Pattern piece D**
*includes 1cm (½in) seam allowance*

**Pattern piece E**
*includes 1cm (½in) seam allowance*

# Index

*Pretty Pocket, page 32.*